# Professor Pete's Prehistoric Animals

# GIANT
# MEAT-EATING
# DINOSAURS

**W**

FRANKLIN WATTS
LONDON•SYDNEY

Franklin Watts
This edition published in the UK in 2017 by The Watts Publishing Group

Copyright © 2013 David West Children's Books

*Designed and illustrated* by David West

ISBN: 978 1 4451 5363 6

Printed in Malaysia

Franklin Watts
An imprint of
Hachette Children's Group
Part of The Watts Publishing Group
Carmelite House
50 Victoria Embankment
London EC4Y 0DZ

An Hachette UK Company.
www.hachette.co.uk

www.franklinwatts.co.uk

PROFESSOR PETE'S PREHISTORIC ANIMALS GIANT MEAT-EATING DINOSAURS
was produced for Franklin Watts by
David West Children's Books, 6 Princeton Court, 55 Felsham Road, London SW15 1AZ

**Professor Pete says:**
This little guy will tell you something more about the animal.

Learn what this animal ate.

Where and when (Mya=Millions of Years Ago) did it live?

Its size is revealed!

How fast or slow was it?

Discover the meaning of its name.

A timeline on page 24 shows you the dates of the different periods in Mya.

# Contents

**Professor Pete says:**
Acrocanthosaurus was a powerful hunter. It had strong arms to hold on to its **prey** while it slashed with its razor-sharp teeth.

# Acrocanthosaurus

ah-kroh-kan-tho-SORE-us

This large, sharp-toothed **predator** hunted giant, long-necked plant eaters that lived in the pine forests of the North American continent.

Acrocanthosaurus was a meat eater and probably fed on large, plant-eating dinosaurs.

It lived in Canada and the United States during the Lower Cretaceous period, 115–105 Mya.

Acrocanthosaurus was about 12 metres in length and weighed 6 tonnes.

It is thought that Acrocanthosaurus could run as fast as 40 kilometres per hour.

Acrocanthosaurus means 'high-spined lizard' after the tall spine bones along its back.

Allosaurus was a meat eater and probably fed on many different types of plant-eating dinosaurs such as the plated Stegosaurus.

It lived in the United States and Tanzania during the Upper Cretaceous period, 153–135 Mya.

Allosaurus grew up to 12 metres in length and weighed 2.3 tonnes.

It could run fast in short bursts, around 32.2 kilometres per hour.

Allosaurus means 'other lizard'.

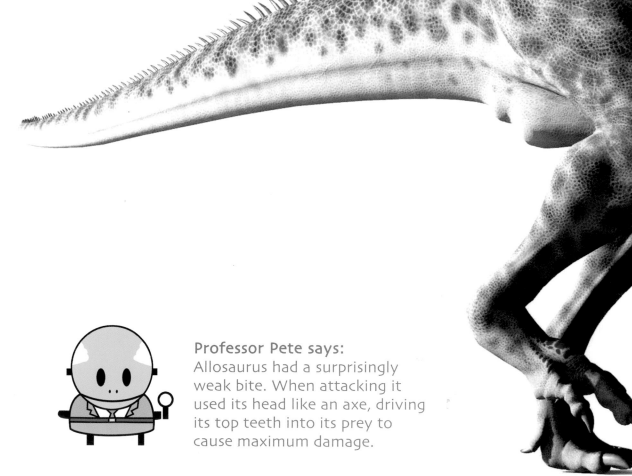

**Professor Pete says:**
Allosaurus had a surprisingly weak bite. When attacking it used its head like an axe, driving its top teeth into its prey to cause maximum damage.

# Allosaurus

AL-oh-saw-russ

This speedy killer was
the most common predator in
North America 140 million years ago.
It hunted on the plains, using
surprise to ambush its prey.

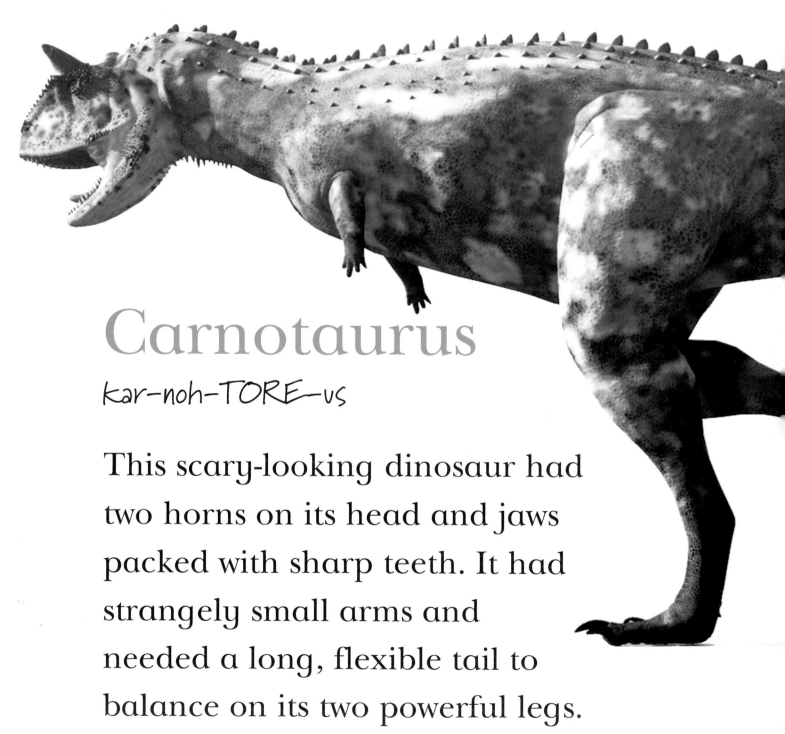

# Carnotaurus

Kar-noh-TORE-us

This scary-looking dinosaur had two horns on its head and jaws packed with sharp teeth. It had strangely small arms and needed a long, flexible tail to balance on its two powerful legs.

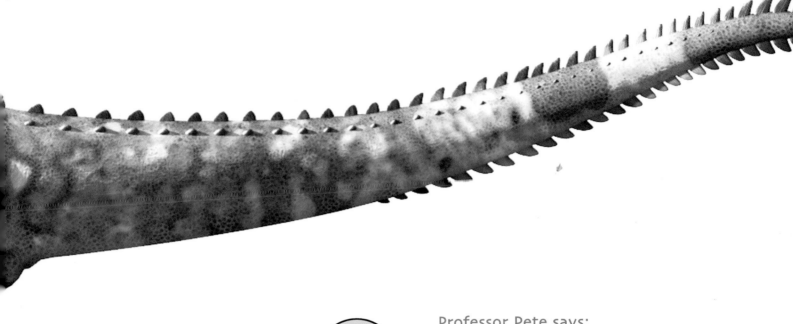

**Professor Pete says:**
The eyes of Carnotaurus faced forwards, which is unusual in a dinosaur. This meant it had eyesight similar to ours, which would have made it a good hunter.

 Carnotaurus was a meat eater and probably fed on smaller plant-eating dinosaurs.

 It lived in South America during the Upper Cretaceous period, 75 Mya.

 Carnotaurus was about 8 metres in length and weighed 1.5–2.4 tonnes.

 Carnotaurus could reach a top speed of 50 kilometres per hour.

 Carnotaurus means 'meat-eating bull', named after the horns on its head.

9

# Cryolophosaurus

cry-o-loaf-o-sore-us

This giant predator hunted plant eaters such as Glacialisaurus in southern lands now called Antarctica.

**Professor Pete says:**
The crest on its head was probably used for display to impress females. It used to be known as Elvisaurus, after Elvis Presley, because its crest looked like a **quiff**.

10

Cryolophosaurus lived in Antarctica during the Lower Jurassic period, 170 Mya.

It was a meat eater and probably fed on plant-eating dinosaurs.

Cryolophosaurus was about 8 metres in length and weighed around 0.9 tonnes.

It could run faster than a Tyrannosaurus, reaching speeds of 50 kilometres per hour.

Cryolophosaurus means 'cold-crest lizard' after its discovery in cold Antarctica and the crest on its head.

11

Giganotosaurus was a meat eater and fed on giant, long-necked, plant-eating dinosaurs.

 It lived in Argentina during the Upper Cretaceous period, 97 Mya.

 Giganotosaurus was about 13 metres in length and weighed 5.4 tonnes.

 Giganotosaurus could reach a speed of 50 kilometres per hour.

 Giganotosaurus means 'giant southern lizard'.

# Giganotosaurus

gig-an-OH-toe-SORE-us

Giganotosaurus was one of the biggest of the giant meat eaters. This massive predator hunted the plains of South America for large, long-necked **titanosaurs**.

**Professor Pete says:**
For such a large beast, Giganotosaurus had a surprisingly small brain, the size and shape of a banana.

**Professor Pete says:**
Fossil evidence has
shown that these
ferocious dinosaurs
fought to the death
and ate each other.

Majungasaurus was a meat eater and fed on plant-eating dinosaurs such as Rapetosaurus.

It lived in Madagascar during the Upper Cretaceous period, 84–71 Mya.

Majungasaurus was about 6 metres in length and weighed 1.1 tonnes.

Majungasaurus was slower than some predators, reaching a speed of 32.2 kilometres per hour.

Majungasaurus was named after the place where it was found, Mahajanga, in Madagascar.

# Majungasaurus

mah-joong-gah-SORE-us

Majungasaurus was a medium-sized predator with a strong, stocky build. It used its powerful jaws to hang on to its prey until it stopped struggling.

15

# Spinosaurus

SPINE–oh–SORE–us

Spinosaurus is the largest of all the meat-eating dinosaurs. Its skull was long and narrow like a crocodile's, which was ideal for catching its favourite food, fish! It had a large sail on its back that acted like a car's radiator to keep it cool.

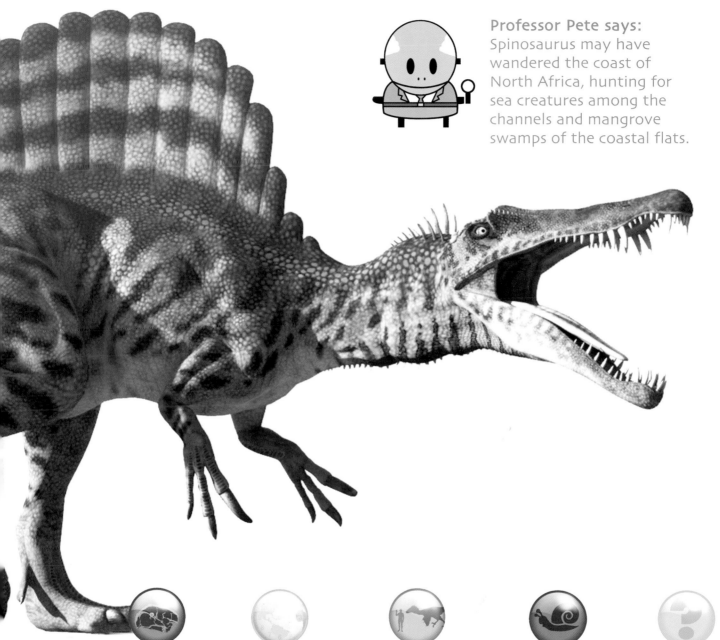

**Professor Pete says:**
Spinosaurus may have wandered the coast of North Africa, hunting for sea creatures among the channels and mangrove swamps of the coastal flats.

This ferocious-looking dinosaur ate fish and other water animals from rivers and lakes.

It lived in North Africa during the Lower to Upper Cretaceous periods, 97 Mya.

Spinosaurus was 12.6–18 metres long and 7–20.9 tonnes in weight.

Spinosaurus could only reach a top speed of about 24 kilometres per hour.

Spinosaurus means 'spine lizard'. It is called this because of the large spines inside its sail.

17

# Suchomimus

sook-oh-mim-us

This dinosaur's snout was similar to a crocodile's. Its jaw, crammed with backwards-pointing teeth, was ideal for catching slippery, wriggling fish!

Suchomimus ate fish and other water animals from rivers and lakes.

It lived in Niger, Africa during the Lower Cretaceous period, 121–112 Mya.

Suchomimus was 11 metres long and 3.6 tonnes in weight.

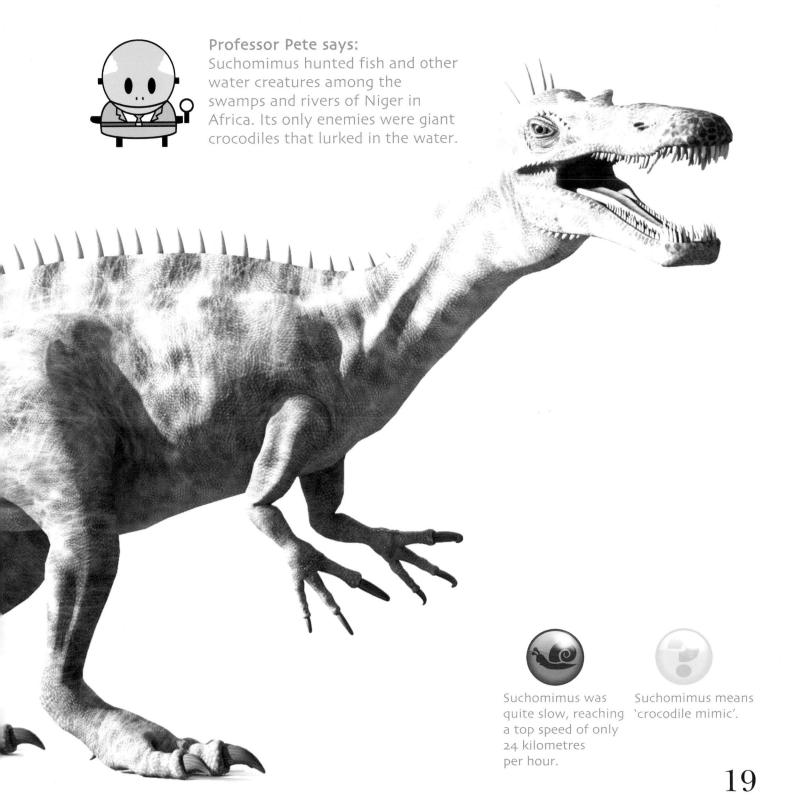

**Professor Pete says:**
Suchomimus hunted fish and other water creatures among the swamps and rivers of Niger in Africa. Its only enemies were giant crocodiles that lurked in the water.

Suchomimus was quite slow, reaching a top speed of only 24 kilometres per hour.

Suchomimus means 'crocodile mimic'.

19

**Professor Pete says:**
Scientists found teeth marks from a
Tarbosaurus on the fossil remains of a
Saurolophus. They worked out that the
Saurolophus was already dead, proving
that Tarbosauruses were also **scavengers**.

Tarbosaurus ate meat. Its favourite meal was Saurolophus.

 It lived in China and Mongolia during the Upper Cretaceous period, 74–60 Mya.

 Tarbosaurus was 10 metres long and 3.6 tonnes in weight.

 Tarbosaurus was quite fast, reaching speeds between 40–72 kilometres per hour.

 Tarbosaurus means 'alarming lizard'.

# Tarbosaurus

TAR-bow-SORE-us

Tarbosaurus was a slightly smaller relative of Tyrannosaurus. It ambushed its prey, running a short distance before delivering a killing bite.

21

Tyrannosaurus ate dinosaurs and even, occasionally, its own kind!

It lived in North America during the Upper Cretaceous period, 67–65.5 Mya.

It measured up to 12.3 metres in length, up to 4 metres tall at the hips, and was up to 6.8 tonnes in weight.

Tyrannosaurus could only reach a top speed of 40 kilometres per hour.

Tyrannosaurus means 'tyrant lizard'.

# Tyrannosaurus

tie-RAN-oh-SORE-us

This dinosaur is the most famous of all. It had a massive skull balanced by a long, heavy tail. It had powerful legs and small arms with two fingers.

# Glossary

**predators**
Animals that hunt other animals for food.

**prey**
An animal that is hunted for food.

**quiff**
Hair on the head that is brushed into a peak.

**scavengers**
Animals that feed on dead matter.

**titanosaurs**
A group of long-necked dinosaurs that included some of the heaviest animals ever to walk the Earth.

# Timeline

Dinosaurs lived during the Mesozoic Era which is divided into three main periods.

| TRIASSIC | JURASSIC | | | CRETACEOUS | |
|---|---|---|---|---|---|
| Upper | Lower | Middle | Upper | Lower | Upper |
| 227 | 205 | 180 | 159 | 144 | 98 | 65 |

Millions of Years Ago (Mya)